# PINK FLOYD

## GLORIOUS TORMENT

Publisher and Creative Director: Nick Wells

Project Editor: Polly Prior

Art Director: Mike Spender

Layout Design: Jane Ashley

Digital Design and Production: Chris Herbert

Special thanks to: Laura Bulbeck, Emma Chafer, Esme Chapman, Anna Groves and Karen Fitzpatrick

**FLAME TREE PUBLISHING**

Crabtree Hall, Crabtree Lane

Fulham, London SW6 6TY

United Kingdom

www.flametreepublishing.com


www.flametreemusic.com


First published 2013


12 14 16 15 13

1 3 5 7 9 10 8 6 4 2


© 2013 Flame Tree Publishing Ltd

A CIP record for this book is available from the British Library upon request.


ISBN 978-0-85775-988-7


Printed in China

# PINK FLOYD

## GLORIOUS TORMENT

### SEAN EGAN

Foreword: Jerry Ewing

Editor, *Classic Rock Presents Prog*

**FLAME TREE
PUBLISHING**

# CONTENTS

# FOREWORD

'Our music is like an abstract painting. It should suggest something to each person,' Syd Barrett once told a reporter. The late, one-time frontman of Pink Floyd was spot-on. Pink Floyd's long and illustrious career has mapped out new and ever further-reaching soundscapes as their career has progressed. From the abstract, psychedelic quirkiness of their 1967 debut album *The Piper At The Gates Of Dawn* all the way through to the analytical overview of the channels of communication that coursed its way through 1994's *The Division Bell*, the band have challenged, questioned and ultimately thrilled listeners for 40 years.

The near hysterical fervour that greeted the decision of David Gilmour, Richard Wright and Nick Mason, to accede to the demands of Bob Geldof to reunite with their erstwhile colleague Roger Waters for 2005's Live 8 performance, over a decade after the band's name was attached to any recorded output, speaks volumes for Pink Floyd's legacy, a sumptuous tapestry draped over rock's effervescent body.

And yet it is somehow equally fitting that this unique and final overture was itself drawn to a perpetual close in an appropriately English and subdued manner with the sad passing of, first, Syd Barrett, in July 2006, who had long retreated from the acid-fuelled Sixties limelight to Cambridge, from whence the band originally came, followed in September 2008 by Rick Wright's sudden and unexpected passing. As much as the final coming together by the perceived 'classic' Floyd line-up took place with little fanfare from the band themselves, so the passing of old colleagues was greeted with quietly dignified tributes.

The band's disinterest in fame has been well documented in the music they have made. It is a suitably English approach from these progenitors of that quintessentially English of music genres, progressive rock. And yet it is this reticence to make overtures to the media that has gone a long way in shrouding the story of Pink Floyd with the cloak of mythology. And much like their music, despite what you think you know, there's always something else to be discovered. Syd Barrett was right, you know.

**Jerry Ewing**

Editor, *Classic Rock Presents Prog*

# PROG
# PIONEERS

'I THINK WE
WERE GREATER
THAN THE SUM
OF OUR PARTS.'
DAVID GILMOUR

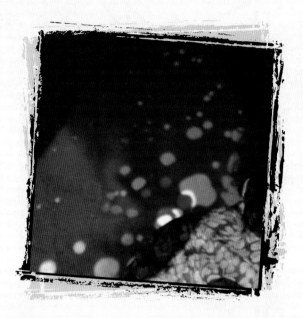

That Pink Floyd became one of the most important rock bands of all time is something of a surprise. Not that their music wasn't marked by a tremendous depth of quality or that they didn't make ceaseless innovations on both record and stage; rather it's surprising because from the beginning they were distinctly un-rock.

## Comfortable Backgrounds

For a start, they were undeniably middle class. Although they came into being in London, their nucleus hailed from Cambridge, an English town that is a byword for culture and academia. Their mostly comfortable family backgrounds, well-spoken Home Counties tones and – Roger Waters excepted – lack of any chips on their shoulders were things still pretty much considered to be the antithesis of rock'n'roll's working-class, rebellious spirit.

## Who Are Ya?

Further undermining their rock-star credibility was their facelessness. In 1994, paparazzi awaiting Pink Floyd at an Italian airport were left standing around long after their quarry had slipped out under their noses. It was symptomatic of the fact that few people would recognize the group's members if they passed them in the street. With the exception of a period surrounding their first few releases, Floyd made their music the star, never themselves. Part of this involved taking popular music places it had never been before. Their innovations with lighting, effects and props proved that rock could be an awesome spectacle and all-round experience rather than a matter of glamorous entertainers strutting around the stage.

## Lordly Rockers

Their third supposed demerit was that they were never very interested in uptempo songs. Rock is supposed to be about speed and the sweaty excitement that its four-beats-to-the-bar metre generates. In the whole of Pink Floyd's recorded catalogue – well over a hundred songs – you would be hard-pressed to find a dozen tracks deserving the description 'rocker'. Yet this no more caused them to be perceived as interlopers on the rock scene than their lack of working-class backgrounds or their anonymity. Stately their grooves may have been, but implicit in all of them was a love of the same classic rock'n'roll records in their fans' collections.

'WE WERE ONE OF THE FIRST BANDS TO BENEFIT FROM THE FREEDOM THAT THE BEATLES HAD PROVIDED.'

NICK MASON

## Floyd Times Three

Remarkably, the story of Pink Floyd is the story of three very different bands. The first was a short-lived but hugely influential ensemble led by Syd Barrett. The only member of Floyd who could ever have been described as charismatic, Barrett nailed the band's colours firmly to the kaleidoscopic mast of psychedelia. After his departure, Floyd dispensed with the whimsical and gimmicky elements of psychedelia but retained its penchant for improvisation, experimentation and elongation. This combination of the grit of rock, the audacious conceptualization of the *avant garde* and the extended majesty of classical music came to be known as progressive rock – and Floyd were the new genre's kings. A third permutation of the group after chief songwriter Roger Waters' departure is dismissed by many as a footnote to the real group's story but achieved undeniably colossal commercial success.

Pink Floyd are no more, but the tidal wave of emotion that greeted their brief onstage reunion in 2005 is a measure of how they overcame all the preconceptions about their origins and methods to become one of music's enduring legends.

'Our sense of snotty purity was so great that we wouldn't even have a single out.'

Roger Waters

'PINK FLOYD HAS ALWAYS BEEN THE THINKING MAN'S ROCK'N' ROLL.'

# THE DAWN OF PINK FLOYD

**D**rummer Nick Mason (born in 1944 in Birmingham, raised in Hampstead) thought he had put music behind him when he began an architecture course at London's Regent Street Polytechnic in 1962. However, fellow student Roger Waters (born in 1943 in Surrey but raised in Cambridge) got him interested in his band Sigma 6.

## Awkward But Gifted

The death of Waters' father when he was four months old had a profound effect on him. Also leaving a deep imprint was his schooling: education in Britain in the post-war period was brutally authoritarian and Waters' secondary school, Cambridge County High School for Boys, seems to have been among the worst. Perhaps these traumas are what accounts

'IT'S DEFINITELY A COMPLETE REALISATION OF THE AIMS OF PSYCHEDELIA.'
ROGER WATERS

'OUR MUSIC IS LIKE AN ABSTRACT PAINTING. IT SHOULD SUGGEST SOMETHING TO EACH PERSON.'

SYD BARRETT

# 'HE WAS THE KEY THAT UNLOCKED THE DOOR TO ROCK 'N' ROLL FOR ME.'

for the fact that Waters is the exception to the band members' extraordinary niceness. He is the archetypal temperamental artist: overly proprietorial of the band's name and product; prone to treating other members as his backing musicians; and not unknown for terminating relationships with people for whom he feels he has no further use.

However, there is no denying that Waters is the most important member in Floyd's history. As well as a swaggering ego he possessed a driving ambition that continually pushed the band to new heights, and his songs and visions gave the band an identity that was particularly important in light of their facelessness.

Sigma 6's keyboardist initially only played if venues boasted a piano. Named Richard Wright, he was born in 1943 in Middlesex, raised in Harrow, and differed academically from Mason and Waters in that he had switched from an architecture to a music course. The band's name evolved to The Abdabs, thence to The Screaming Abdabs, thence to The Tea Set.

## The Crucial Element

The band really came into focus with the arrival of guitarist and vocalist Roger 'Syd' Barrett. Born in Cambridge in 1946, when he joined the band he was studying art in Camberwell. His recruitment saw Waters demoted from guitar to bass.

Barrett only played on one full Pink Floyd album, yet he is crucial to the history of the band. Indeed, many an original Floyd follower will tell you that Pink Floyd without him was merely a group flying a flag of convenience purveying music that had nothing to do with the Barrett vision, and that he alone was responsible for the band's legendary status.

## Bluesy Pink Name

When another band with the name The Tea Set was discovered, again a name change was required. Like many musicians in Britain in the mid-Sixties, the group were keen to assert their blues credentials, yet there is scant blues (as opposed to rhythm & blues) influence discernible in any of their recordings. Nor were they known for knocking out renditions of the likes of 'Mannish Boy' or 'Rollin' and Tumblin'' on stage. In deciding to go out under a title that was a conflation of Pink Anderson and Floyd Council – two blues practitioners so obscure that barely any of the blues and R&B ensembles in the British Isles had any of their songs in their sets – they seem to have been over-compensating.

Even the new moniker was subject to an evolutionary process: it was initially The Pink Floyd Sound (and even when shortened was for many years colloqiually The Pink Floyd). They made their debut under the Floyd handle at the Countdown Club in late 1965.

# FOR THE LOVE OF ROCK

'I ACTUALLY
LEARNED THE
GUITAR WITH
THE HELP OF A
PETE SEEGER
INSTRUCTIONAL
RECORD WHEN
I WAS 13 OR 14.'
DAVID GILMOUR

Like all bands, Pink Floyd were inspired by artists who came before them. However, it's very difficult to pinpoint their influences by listening to their music: the work of the people they admired was diluted to the point of invisibility once refracted through the prism of their singular techniques.

## The Usual Suspects

Their early musical fumblings are the familiar-verging-on-banal story of most aspiring British artists of their generation: socks knocked off by Elvis and Dylan, inspired by The Beatles into thinking that stardom could be theirs, starting to gig with a mixture of pop hits and R&B standards.

There were differences, though. The style of Wright, for instance, was not characterized by the pumping insistence of rock but the spatial, glistening properties of a jazz keyboardist, as befitting a man in love with Miles Davis' classic 1959 *Kind Of Blue* album.

## Studiedly English

The Kinks bequeathed Floyd their unusual vocal style, Barrett taking heart from the way that Ray Davies unfashionably sang in his native accent and still found favour. Although Barrett's decision was wrapped up in the studiedly whimsical Englishness of psychedelia; his successor David Gilmour carried on his vocal approach in a less self-conscious style.

Blues-rock trio Cream were an inspiration for Mason. He wrote in his memoir of being impressed by the fact that they relied purely on their musical power: 'No need to dress in Beatle jackets and tab-collar shirts, and no need to have a good-looking singer….'

Gilmour was a huge fan of Jimi Hendrix. Not only did he adopt a Fender Stratocaster in emulation, but he found Jimi's wild guitar explorations sufficiently inspiring to put aside his personal humility and essentially tear up the joint on tracks like 'The Nile Song' and 'Fat Old Sun'.

As nice middle-class boys, that the group members would have heard a lot more classical music than most of their musical peers had clearly had an impact. Additionally, in their early days Floyd

# 'HIS IMPACT ON MY THINKING WAS ENORMOUS. A MAJOR REGRET IS THAT I NEVER GOT TO KNOW HIM.'

DAVID BOWIE ON SYD BARRETT

were particularly enthralled by the experimental art-music of German composer Karlheinz Stockhausen, pioneer of electronic music and musical spatialization.

These disparate and unusual influences showed when future co-manager Peter Jenner saw Floyd play at the Marquee in 1966: '... during very straightforward blues songs ... they would go off into these psychedelic interludes,' he marvelled.

The stage was set for Pink Floyd to take the world by storm, but on their own thoughtful, exploratory terms. Their glittering career would see them in turn influence a new generation of musicians.

## Massively Pervasive Model

Just as it's difficult to spot Floyd's influences in their output, so there are few records to which one can point and confidently assert that they would not exist without them. However, it's fair to conclude that prog-rock contemporaries like Genesis and Yes admired what they did; David Bowie was given the courage to plunge into his *avant garde* Berlin Trilogy by their work, Radiohead's well-educated miserabilism was presaged by them and Orbital's ambient exercises are in debt to them.

What can be stated without a doubt is that the number of homes containing a copy of Floyd's masterpiece *The Dark Side Of The Moon* – reputed to be the third biggest-selling album in history – is a measure of just how massively pervasive and potent their musical model was.

'SYD WAS INFLUENCED BY JOHN LENNON, PARTICULARLY LENNON'S RESENTMENT OF THE POP MACHINE.'

NICK MASON ON SYD BARRETT

# SPONTANEOUS UNDERGROUND

'WE WERE USELESS. WE COULDN'T PLAY AT ALL SO WE HAD TO DO SOMETHING STUPID AND "EXPERIMENTAL".'
ROGER WATERS

**N**ew boy he might have been, but the strength of Syd Barrett's personality (however eccentric) and, in time, the power of his original compositions made him the group's de facto leader.

## Pioneering By Accident

When Pink Floyd secured a residency at London's Marquee Club in early 1966, it led to an approach that would come to define the band. Realizing they didn't know enough songs to play their allotted stage time, they began extending and improvising. In the context of the era, this was seen as a quasi-political statement: rebelling against the three-minute strictures of the suits who ran the radio playlists. Their accidental pioneering meant they began to build a following.

> ‘IF WE HAVE TO HAVE SOME KIND OF DEFINITION, YOU COULD SAY THE PINK FLOYD WERE LIGHTS AND SOUNDS.’
>
> ROGER WATERS

By the end of the year, hoary covers of the likes of 'Louie Louie' and 'Roadrunner' had been replaced in their repertoire by originals. Their stage act acquired another signature as a result of their fundraising dates in October and November at the London Free School's Sound And Light Workshop. An American couple named Joel and Toni Brown used a slide projector to provide the band with a makeshift light show. Hitherto, a spotlight or two was the extent of the effects to which audiences were treated.

October 1966 saw Floyd play at the launch party for what would become the hippy bible, *International Times*. At a gig that has gone down in legend, they enraptured two thousand people – including celebrity guests like Paul McCartney – at London's Roundhouse. Spotlights flashed to Mason's drumbeats and the volume was such that the power failed.

## Getting It Together

That same month, the band assumed a semblance of professionalism when they formed Blackhill Enterprises with their new managers Peter Jenner and Andrew King. One of the first things the pair did was to buy the band a thousand pounds' worth of equipment – approximately £16,000 in today's money. It was promptly stolen. Had it not been for a gift of £200 from Mason's mum and the benefits of hire purchase, Floyd's career might have ended there and then. Come December, though, they were the house band at a

'THERE IS PROBABLY MORE CO-ORDINATION BETWEEN US THAN ANY OTHER POP GROUP. WE PLAY LIKE A JAZZ GROUP.'

RICHARD WRIGHT

# CRAZY DIAMOND

'THE PINK FLOYD
... ARE NOT
TRYING TO
CREATE
HALLUCINATORY
EFFECTS ON THEIR
AUDIENCES.'
EMI PRESS RELEASE

**P**olydor had expressed interest in signing the group but it was EMI who eventually secured their services. Curiously they made them perform a 30-minute audition even though the contracts had been signed and sealed.

## A New Kind Of Pop

Some UFO Club regulars thought 'Arnold Layne' a sell-out: the song was brightly melodic and short, with only Wright's elongated celestial organ solo differentiating it musically from the usual hit-parade fare. However, it was assuredly the first single about someone with this 'strange hobby' to make the airwaves and although the band promoted it in the *de rigueur* fashions of the season – exotically patterned shirts, neckerchiefs, candy stripes and so on – the accompanying

'IT'S SAD IN A WAY ... BECAUSE IT REMINDS ME OF WHAT MIGHT HAVE BEEN.'

RICHARD WRIGHT ON THE PIPER AT THE GATES OF DAWN

film they devised was not standard stuff. It depicted them not miming the lyric and frolicking on a beach with a clothes dummy – which as with all unadorned dummies somehow seemed obscene in its nakedness. The single reached No. 20 in the UK chart and far-out Floyd now found themselves in the mainstream.

Certainly, the mums and dads of many of their new fans wouldn't have allowed them to attend the 14-hour 'Technicolour Dream' at Alexandra Palace in April at which the band were one of the main attractions. They missed quite an event, one that is recorded as perhaps even more legendary than the *International Times* launch party.

## Barrett's Finest Moment

Barrett wrote a new song called 'Games For May' especially for a concert of the same name held at the Queen Elizabeth Hall on 12 May 1967. All this neat conceptuality was dispensed with when Barrett reworked the song and re-christened it 'See Emily Play'. When the group recorded it at EMI's studios in Abbey Road, they were not impressed with the sound engendered by the plush facility and went back to Sound Techniques to re-record it.

'See Emily Play' is probably Barrett's greatest song. Again, it was catchy and short, but it was pop on its own terms. A depiction of a posh flower-child embracing experiences of which her bourgeois parents most certainly would not have approved, it possessed a nursery-rhyme quality and a spiritual

# A NEW BEGINNING

'COULDN'T
CARE LESS.
ALL WE CAN
DO IS MAKE
RECORDS
WHICH
WE LIKE.'
SYD BARRETT
ON THE
FAILURE OF
'APPLES AND
ORANGES'

**P**iper was the final artistic statement of a fully functioning Syd Barrett. No sooner had he announced his talent to the world than he started on a precipitous mental descent. Barrett's generation had assumed that LSD was harmless, but his experiences proved one of the first indications of how harmful it could be.

## The Worst Trip Of All

The early signs were subtle and could be dismissed as a bad trip or a tantrum. But the mental deterioration increased through 1967 as Floyd embarked on their first US tour, participated in a UK package tour headlined by The Jimi Hendrix Experience, promoted their third single 'Apples And Oranges' (a surprising flop) and played the star-studded

'I DON'T LIKE THE SONG OR THE WAY IT'S SUNG.'

ROGER WATERS ON SINGLE 'IT WOULD BE SO NICE'

# 'THERE ARE ONE OR TWO THINGS IN SYD'S STYLE THAT I KNOW CAME FROM ME.'

DAVID GILMOUR ON SYD BARRETT'S GUITAR TECHNIQUE

Christmas On Earth gig. Throughout this, Barrett variously failed to sing, play, tune his guitar properly or be in a fit state to even attempt a performance. When David Gilmour was recruited as a second guitarist in January 1968 in order to prevent the band's stock plummeting further, the writing was on the wall. Barrett's departure was officially announced in April and the band continued as a four-piece.

Despite the legions of Barrett devotees who would insist otherwise, even had Barrett not been stricken by mental ill-health, his continued presence in the band wouldn't have enabled them to become the legend they did. Notwithstanding his considerable talents or the fact that Floyd never opted for the conventional, Barrett's approach was just too eccentric and rooted in the passing fad of psychedelia to be truly sustainable.

## Enter The Nice Guy

His replacement was an old mate of the band's. Not only had Floyd often shared bills with his group Joker's Wild, Gilmour had even taught Barrett some guitar riffs back when they both attended Cambridge Technical College. Gilmour was born just outside Cambridge in 1946.

Gilmour is often positioned as the man in the white hat in contrast to Roger Waters' bad guy. The band's guitarist and for a long time lead vocalist is polite and quietly spoken. However, he has his pompous side: journalists have been known to be briefed by his PR people not to address him as 'Dave'.

Although Gilmour has never been as prolific in his songwriting nor as visionary as Waters, his exhilarating, mellifluous guitar work is the instrumental ying to the yang of Waters' lyrics – not least because Floyd have, more than most bands, given lyrics a backseat to music.

## A Shaky New Start

Steve O'Rourke became the newly leader-less Floyd's manager and remained so until his death in 2003. His charges began their post-Barrett career very uncertainly. 'It Would Be So Nice' was a single written and sung by Wright. Not only was it so self-consciously Syd-like as to almost seem designed to fool people into thinking that Barrett was still in the ranks, it flopped. Floyd's contributions to the soundtrack of arthouse film *The Committee* were heard by few.

Things began to turn around in June. That month saw their headlining last-day appearance at the Hyde Park Free Festival well received, something that can also be said for their second album, *A Saucerful Of Secrets*, released at the same time.

# CELESTIAL VOICES

'IT WOULD HAVE BEEN A BETTER ALBUM IF WE'D GONE AWAY, DONE THE THINGS, COME BACK TOGETHER.'
ROGER WATERS ON UMMAGUMMA

lthough vocals were shared, the issue of who would replace Barrett as musical visionary was indicated by the fact that *A Saucerful Of Secrets'* lovely opener 'Let There Be More Light' and its instantly iconic and live favourite 'Set The Controls For The Heart Of The Sun' were both Waters compositions.

## Barrett Takes A Bow

The album ended symbolically with a Barrett composition and vocal. The parping brass and confessional tone of 'Jugband Blues' was completely at odds with the rest of the record's sleekness but it served as Barrett's sign-off to the band he had once commanded. Another effective capstone to the Syd era was the group's appearance in Peter

Whitehead's 1967 documentary 'Tonite Let's All Make Love In London', in which the original band's space-age jamming is captured for posterity.

## A Perfect Storm

*Saucerful* marked the start of the group's long association with Storm Thorgerson, whose sleeve designs would not only make their covers stand out but would also provide another aspect of the band's identity in place of a conventional rock group public image. The band allowed no interference in his designs from their record company, even though the latter would naturally have been worried that Floyd's name, faces and album title rarely made the covers. This prioritising of art over commerce was in keeping with Floyd's concurrent decision to take a reduced royalty rate in exchange for unlimited studio time.

Although Floyd had of course shown a penchant for extended pieces and improvisation with Barrett in the band, his departure only moved them further in that direction: at that point, nobody in their ranks had his ability to write three-minute, radio-friendly pop singles. The failure of worthy December 1968 single 'Point Me At The Sky' confirmed this. From hereon, vocals would be less important on Floyd records and there would be no UK single for more than a decade. The latter strategy, along with the fact that they now rarely consented to interviews, served to create a mystique about Floyd.

# 'I DON'T REALLY LIKE WORKING UNDER THAT SORT OF PRESSURE, BUT IT CAN HELP YOU BY FOCUSING YOUR IDEAS.'

## A Strange Success

Their snowballing live reputation would seem to be partly due to the fact that half of double-set *Ummagumma* (1969) was an in-concert recording. It was a bit presumptuous for a group with only two full albums to their name to be taking the route of issuing live versions of previously released songs. (*More* [1969] went Top 10 and was pretty good but as it was a soundtrack was not considered a 'real' Floyd album.) However, the live portion of the album was well received. Not so the studio tracks, which saw all four members working in isolation to compile ('write' doesn't seem a fitting description) meandering sounds ('songs' doesn't feel particularly appropriate either). It seems astonishing from this end of history that the album was a commercial success, making No. 5 in the UK.

## Moving Into Their Pomp

*Atom Heart Mother* (1969) was much more like it. From its talking-point cover photograph of a huge, lugubrious cow to its side-long sweeping suite, to its pastoral second side, it revealed a band about to enter their pomp.

*Meddle* (1971) featured another side-long suite in the form of 'Echoes'. The album was the first on which the band had worked as a whole since *A Saucerful Of Secrets* and the first to be entirely produced by themselves. The record saw the band alternate bizarre sound experiments with supreme listenability.

'OTHER GROUPS WOULD BE QUITE HORRIFIED IF THEY SAW HOW WE REALLY WASTE OUR RECORDING TIME.'

ROGER WATERS

little in the way of lyrics makes the fact that it topped the charts worldwide not that surprising. However, the cycle of public opinion soon turned harshly against such music and by the end of the decade millions were left wondering how they could ever have found listenable other notable prog rock works like *Brain Salad Surgery* by Emerson, Lake and Palmer or *Selling England By The Pound* by Genesis. No such revisionist fate for *The Dark Side Of The Moon.* Even though some of its original allure was dependent on the novelty of its high-tech effects, it continues to be regarded as a classic.

## The Experimental Pop Record

With this album, Floyd married experimentalism and commercialism. It made perfect sense for an album dominated by long instrumental passages to be perceived as populist simply because the music was so divine that it struck a chord with the masses. Clare Torry's soulful wailing on 'The Great Gig In The Sky' and the taut, instantly catchy anthem of 'Money' were nothing if not pop.

Although to some extent a laid-back album – it was certainly the preferred soundtrack for the marijuana-smoking students of the day – it also saw Floyd dispensing with their soft side, exchanging the science fiction, romantic and rural fantasies for darker themes of cynicism and alienation. As usual, the cover was unforgettable: the title and the band name were nowhere in evidence but Storm Thorgerson's iconic picture of light going through a triangular prism makes the album instantly recognizable.

# 'ROGER WORKED ALL SORTS OF HOURS ON THE CONCEPT AND THE LYRICS WHILE THE REST OF US WENT HOME...'

DAVID GILMOUR ON DARK SIDE

Floyd's first American Top 40 album, *Dark Side* climbed to No. 1 and remained in the US chart for 591 consecutive weeks. Despite a similarly nigh-on permanent residence in the UK chart, the album amazingly never topped it, peaking at No. 2. 'Money' was released as a single Stateside, making No. 13.

## The Impossible Follow-Up

After abandoning three songs from sessions designed to create an album based on sounds made from household objects, Floyd issued *Wish You Were Here* (1975), previewed at Knebworth in July that year in front of 100,000 people. Considering that *Dark Side* was one of those albums impossible to top, their follow-up was very impressive. Indeed, it's the album that people who can't stand Pink Floyd like. It was stately, classy and seamlessly incorporated saxophone and additional synthesiser into their usual sound. Not only that, it was suffused with a humanity sometimes absent from their work, thanks to the affectionate tribute to Barrett in 'Shine On You Crazy Diamond' and the liltingly beautiful title track. The contents were done justice by Thorgerson's stunning cover photo of a man on fire calmly shaking hands.

# 'HE WANTED TO ... SAY EXACTLY WHAT HE WANTED FOR THE FIRST TIME.'

DAVID GILMOUR ON ROGER WATERS' DARK SIDE LYRICS

'THE ONLY
REASON WE
STAYED
TOGETHER
AFTER WAS
FEAR AND
AVARICE.'
ROGER
WATERS
ON THE
DARK SIDE
OF THE
MOON

# AGAINST THE WALL

'WITH THE
BENEFIT OF
HINDSIGHT
I FOUND
IT A BIT
WHINGING.'
DAVID GILMOUR
ON THE WALL

**O**nly two of *Wish You Were Here's* five songs were credited to Waters alone. However, the collaborative process of that and previous albums was to become a thing of the past.

## A Selfish Socialist?

Waters, a lifelong socialist, had lots of things to get off his chest about a class-ridden British society mired in financial crisis. He was also a forceful personality. Accordingly, only one of the five tracks on *Animals* (1977) featured a compositional credit to any member besides him. He softened the album's political barbs by framing them with Parts I and II of sweet love song 'Pigs On The Wing'. Another instantly iconic sleeve depicted an inflatable pig flying over London landmark Battersea Power Station.

As with many established bands in 1976/77, Floyd had to endure the wrath of the punks, who loudly despised them for their alleged corporatism. A decade after Floyd had been at the centre of the brave new anti-establishment world of London's underground movement, Johnny Rotten – frontman of punk's standard bearers The Sex Pistols – was walking around London in a customized Pink Floyd T-shirt, on which he'd written 'I HATE' above the band's name. That they were a byword for self-indulgence (long songs) and pretension (two Spitfires were booked to fly overhead at Knebworth) was compounded in 1978 when Floyd fled to different parts of the world to escape Britain's tax rate of 83 per cent.

## Self-Disgust = *Magnum Opus*

As with most established groups, the punk disapproval didn't make any difference to their vast popularity. However, it was that popularity that made Waters reassess the value of what he and his colleagues were doing. When Floyd dragged their generators, projection screens and inflatables around the world from January to July 1977 in the vast stadiums where the rock aristocracy ruled, Waters began to hate it all, finding larger audiences unwilling to quietly contemplate the finer details of Floyd's art and even mistaking auxiliary musicians for group members. It culminated in him spitting in an over-eager fan's face.

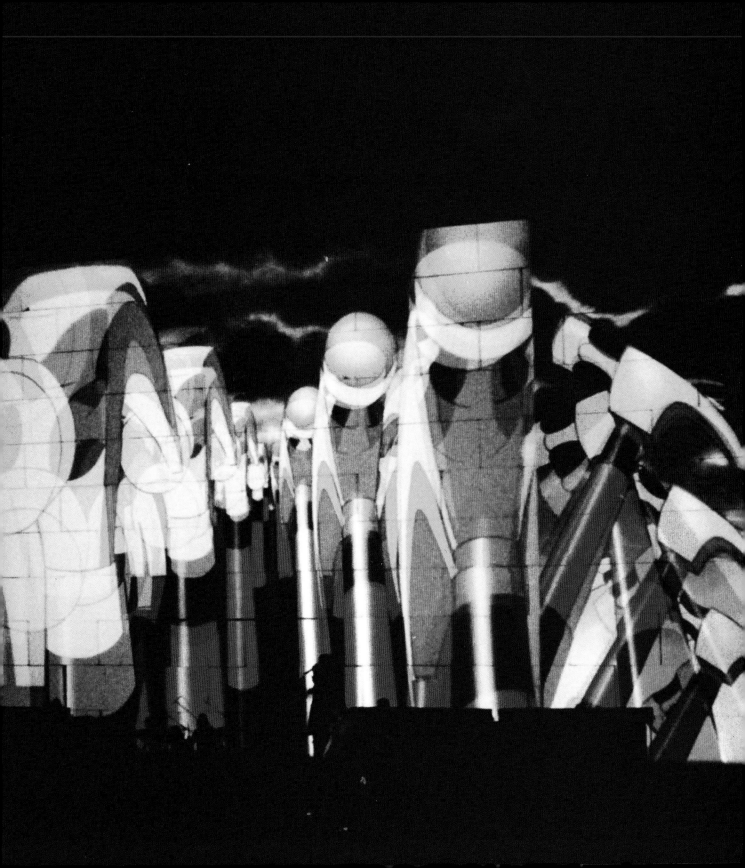

# 'WITHOUT 'PIGS ON THE WING', ANIMALS WOULD HAVE JUST BEEN A KIND OF SCREAM OF RAGE.'

ROGER WATERS

Although he was disgusted with himself, it didn't prevent him exploiting the incident for what became his *magnum opus*. With double-album *The Wall* (1979), Waters – as the character Pink – explored subjects like loss, war and his relationship with his audience. He had so much to say that he overturned all Floydian traditions, packing the songs with lyrics and keeping their running length below four, three and even two minutes.

## Pop Stars All Over Again

Despite the dark themes, the project yielded Floyd's first UK hit single since 'See Emily Play' a dozen years before. When 'Another Brick In The Wall Part 2' was plucked from the album, its funky rhythm and singalong 'We don't need no edu-cay-shun!' chorus caused it to storm to No. 1 on both sides of the Atlantic. Other iconic tracks were 'Is There Anybody Out There?' and 'Comfortably Numb'.

It was absolutely typical of Floyd that when they became hit merchants in a day and age when visuals were increasingly important, they maintained their facelessness. The video for 'Another Brick' that played on millions of TV sets at no point revealed to the public – many of whom had never knowingly heard a Floyd track – what they looked like. Instead they were treated to a surreal animation by Gerald Scarfe and shadowed, chanting schoolchildren.

'IT'S VERY DIFFICULT TO PERFORM IN THAT SITUATION ... IT WAS A SITUATION THAT WE HAVE CREATED OURSELVES OUT OF OUR OWN GREED.'

ROGER WATERS ON LARGE, RESTIVE CROWDS

# A SPENT FORCE?

'I MUST HAVE
COMPLETELY
BLANKED OUT
MY ANGER
AND HURT.'
RICHARD
WRIGHT ON
AGREEING TO
TOUR THE WALL

**S**uch was *The Wall's* abundant success that in 1982 it was even turned into a movie, with Alan Parker directing and Bob Geldof taking the role of Pink. Yet *The Wall's* triumph was actually the beginning of the end.

## Wrighting On The Wall

During the making of *The Wall*, Waters had become dominant to the point of Pink Floyd no longer being a group. Not only had he ousted Gilmour from his position as main vocalist, he had – according to co-producer Bob Ezrin – treated the others as his backing band. Gilmour only got songs on the album at Ezrin's insistence (without which we would have been denied

'Comfortably Numb'). Waters even fired Richard Wright for lack of productivity, although the fact that Wright agreed to help tour the album in a salaried role and the 3½-year gap before the next album initially disguised his dismissal.

Although it could be argued that Waters had proven his importance to the band – not only was *The Wall* brilliant but it also remained at No. 1 in the US for 15 weeks – *The Final Cut* (1983) saw him behaving like some of the megalomaniacs lambasted in his recent songs. All of the 12 tracks were written by him, all but one were exclusively sung by him, he brought in various session musicians and the subject matter seemed tiresomely like another plunge into the sort of neuroses he had plumbed at length and depth on *The Wall*.

## The Final Straw

The album addressed issues stemming from the Falklands War and the questioning at the time of the validity of the welfare state, both instigated by the Margaret Thatcher-led government he despised. It may be somewhat wearing, but does have its fans. Certainly, the glitzy, selfish Eighties was lacking in such works of social conscience. Moreover, 'Not Now John' proved that Floyd could rock out with the best of them.

# '[ROGER] COULD NOT TOLERATE ANYONE ELSE HAVING ANY REAL SAY IN WHAT WAS GOING ON.'

DAVID GILMOUR ON THE FINAL CUT

Floyd had long been used to bad reviews, especially in post-punk Britain, so the slatings of *The Final Cut* were irrelevant. However, the artistic failure of the record was compounded by the fact that with three million sales, it shifted 20 million fewer units than *The Wall*.

## The Floyd Fans' Worst Fears

The absence of Wright's name on *The Final Cut* sleeve was compounded by the abandonment of plans to tour the album. When in March 1984 Gilmour toured to promote his second solo album in contrast to the lack of live dates attending his first solo work's release, it seemed to Floyd's fans like their worst suspicions were true.

Two months later, Waters released his first proper solo album, *The Pros And Cons Of Hitch Hiking*. Waters actually presented this song cycle to his Floyd colleagues at the same time as he laid *The Wall* on them: they had seen more potential in the demos of the latter. What with the fact that Waters deployed much the same group of session musicians as he had on *The Final Cut* and that the subject matter was yet more dark stuff retrieved from Waters' deep well of angst and resentment, it could be perceived as a follow-up to that last Floyd record, only even more underwhelming. When Waters began touring the album in June, he was able to announce the coup that Eric Clapton would be his sideman.

Clapton bailed after the first leg, but Waters seemed sufficiently pleased with his recent work to decide that he and the world no longer needed Pink Floyd.

'THE FINAL CUT WAS ABSOLUTE MISERY TO MAKE. WE WERE ALL FIGHTING LIKE CATS AND DOGS.'
ROGER WATERS

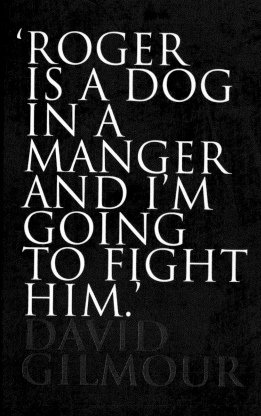

'ROGER
IS A DOG
IN A
MANGER
AND I'M
GOING
TO FIGHT
HIM.'
DAVID
GILMOUR

'THE FINAL CUT WAS ABSOLUTE MISERY TO MAKE. WE WERE ALL FIGHTING LIKE CATS AND DOGS.'
ROGER WATERS

# SIGNS OF LIFE

'NONE OF US HAVE ANY PLANS AT THE MOMENT TO WORK TOGETHER ON ANY PROJECT.'
DAVID GILMOUR ON PINK FLOYD

n 1985, Waters tried to sack manager Steve O'Rourke but couldn't because he was tied into the Pink Floyd company. Waters offered to let the others carry on under the Pink Floyd name if they would release him from the management contract, an offer they apparently declined. In a move startlingly reminiscent of Paul McCartney's motivation for dissolving The Beatles in 1970, to be free of O'Rourke, Waters had no option but to wind up the Pink Floyd company.

## Sue Me, Sue You Blues

In the first week of November 1986, Waters began proceedings in the High Court to dissolve the group 'to maintain the integrity and reputation of the group's name' because he considered it 'a spent force creatively'. EMI

responded with a press release cheerily declaring, 'Pink Floyd is alive, well and recording in England'. EMI's 'up-yours' response was presumably the result of the label having consulted their solicitors and being informed that contractually Waters didn't have a leg to stand on. That certainly seemed to be the case when, in December 1988, it was announced that Waters had concluded his legal dispute with his ex-colleagues in a settlement that allowed them to continue trading as that highly prized Pink Floyd franchise.

Waters' public suggestion that Pink Floyd without him was a 'forgery' must have caused a few wry smiles among the original fans of the band who were outraged back in 1968 to hear that the group were carrying on despite the departure of Syd Barrett.

## Constructing The Forgery

However, it can't be denied that there seems more than a little truth to Waters' characteristically caustic comments. A business-like Gilmour took up Wright's offer to work on a non-Waters Floyd album because 'I thought it would make us stronger legally and musically'. (The salaried Wright was very much a second-class member.) The contributions of Wright and Mason (the latter of whom had been increasingly absent at Floyd sessions in recent years) were so below-par that they were in many cases replaced by the work of session musicians. Gilmour was so unsure of his own writing abilities that he tried

'WE NEVER SAT DOWN AT ANY POINT AND SAID, "IT DOESN'T SOUND FLOYD ENOUGH. MAKE THIS MORE FLOYD."'

DAVID GILMOUR ON MOMENTARY LAPSE

unsuccessfully to work with several lyricists before finally settling on a collaborator in the shape of Anthony Moore. Storm Thorgerson was enlisted to provide an archetypically enigmatic Floydian album cover – an endless sea of hospital beds on a beach – even though the designer hadn't been employed for the last two Floyd albums. You didn't have to be an embittered Waters to conclude that this all raised questions about the meaning and worth of the Floyd brand name. It seemed that the accusations of corporatism by first the music press and then the punks might have some substance to them after all.

## What's In A Name?

The Waters-less *A Momentary Lapse Of Reason* (1987) was a mediocre, self-consciously Floydian work with depressingly fashionable bombastic Eighties production; despite this it went Top 3 both sides of the Atlantic, while Waters' no-worse solo effort *Radio K.A.O.S.* (1987) couldn't crack the Top 20. The tour to promote the Floyd album span off *Delicate Sound Of Thunder* (1988), which sold very respectably for a live album. Clearly, a strong brand was more important than either authenticity or quality.

*'We probably could have resolved it much more amicably by letting Roger out of his management contract.'*

*Nick Mason*

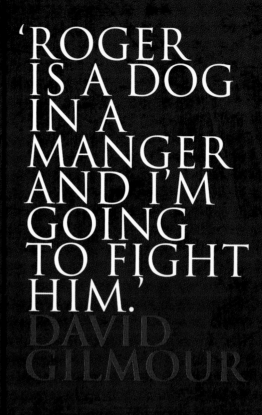

'ROGER IS A DOG IN A MANGER AND I'M GOING TO FIGHT HIM.'

DAVID GILMOUR

# 'I'M COMPETING AGAINST MYSELF AND I'M LOSING.'

ROGER WATERS ON THE TAKINGS OF HIS SOLO TOUR COMPARED TO PINK FLOYD'S

# THE BELL TOLLS

'PINK FLOYD WAS FOUR PEOPLE AND AS THOSE FOUR PEOPLE ARE NO LONGER WORKING TOGETHER, IN MY MIND THAT BAND DOESN'T EXIST ANYMORE.'
ROGER WATERS

**W**hatever one's thoughts about the quality of the Gilmour-led Pink Floyd, it gained a legitimacy simply by its massive success. This process was extended in June 1990 by their headlining the Knebworth Festival.

## Waters Comes Top – For Once

Instances of Waters being able to top his ex-colleagues were few and far between but one such occasion was in July 1990. Waters had once flippantly said that he would only perform *The Wall* again if the Berlin Wall came down. In June 1990, that symbolic destruction of the dividing line between Communism and Capitalism that Waters' generation had never imagined would happen in its lifetime did indeed come to pass. Waters, whose legal settlement with Floyd gave him control over *The Wall*, agreed to stage his masterwork for charity. The event took place on the site of part of the old wall near the Brandenburg Gate at a cost of £4 million. Waters' touring band was augmented by guests like The Scorpions, Sinéad O'Connor, Van Morrison, Tim Curry and Cyndi Lauper. Rumoured appearances by Gilmour and Mason sadly didn't happen. The show – attended by a crowd of 250,000 – span off a live album and video.

Floyd provided the soundtrack to the 1992 film *La Carrera Panamericana*, which documented the motoring race, in which both Gilmour and O'Rourke nearly lost their lives. Fortunately their plunge over a cliff in a C-type Jaguar resulted only in injury. (Mason finished in the first ten.) In April 1992, Pink Floyd received an Ivor Novello songwriting award for Outstanding Contribution to British Music.

## Seven-Year Hitch

Pink Floyd took seven years to produce another studio album. The presence of a Roger Waters-sized hole aside, this time around, its genesis had far more of a smack of authenticity, with Gilmour, Mason and Wright working together on material from the beginning and reverting to the method of generating ideas

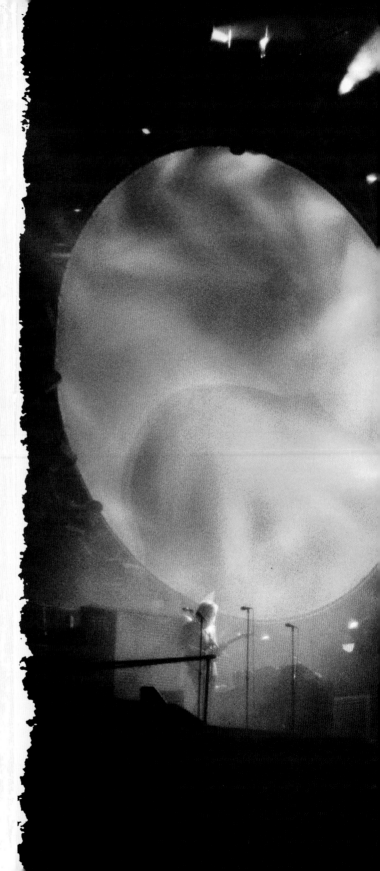

through jamming that had led to some of their best Seventies albums. On the other hand, Gilmour now had to turn to his girlfriend Polly Samson for help with lyrics, a scenario which provoked inevitable ridicule and invocation of the names of Yoko Ono and Linda McCartney. Floyd even had to turn to an outside source – author Douglas Adams – for an album title. Although the best thing about *The Division Bell* (1994) was probably its typically striking Storm Thorgerson cover, it was a respectable enough effort whose unexpected highlight was Wright's co-written 'Wearing The Inside Out'. Its sales were paltry compared to the likes of *The Dark Side Of The Moon* and *The Wall*, but it achieved the psychologically important feat of being the first Pink Floyd album to top the charts on both sides of the Atlantic.

## End Of The Lucrative Road

Thanks partly to the budget provided by corporate sponsor Volkswagen, the tour to promote *The Division Bell* was arguably the most impressive and unarguably the most profitable Floyd excursion yet (it was music's highest grossing tour of all time). It ended with a residency at London's Earl's Court, all profits from which were donated to charity.

Despite the success of the Gilmour-led Pink Floyd, the momentum they had created was allowed to dribble away. That *The Division Bell* turned out to be the end of group activity did rather seem an acknowledgment that, however many people were prepared to sample their wares, the post-Waters Floyd was not the full package.

'WITH ALL DUE RESPECT TO THE PEOPLE WHO WENT OUT AND BOUGHT THOSE RECORDS, THEY ARE JUST RUBBISH.'

ROGER WATERS ON THE GILMOUR-LED FLOYD

'I DON'T WANT TO BE A FULL-TIME MEMBER OF PINK FLOYD ALL MY LIFE. THE AMBITION STAGE OF OUR CAREER IS KIND OF BEHIND US.'

DAVID GILMOUR

# THE SHOW MUST GO ON

'WITH THE AMOUNT OF TECHNOLOGY UP ON STAGE THESE DAYS, YOU'VE GOT TO HAVE YOUR WITS ABOUT YOU.'
DAVID GILMOUR

Joel and Toni Brown didn't know what they were starting in 1966 when they generated a light show with a slide projector. Pink Floyd loved the surreal ambience created by having coloured lights washing across their faces and before long were the first band to travel with a light show.

## Beautiful Sights And Sounds

As the technology and budgets improved, progressively they cranked up the total immersive experience of a Pink Floyd concert, incorporating Hollywood-like special effects and film projections. Thus a band with no Mick Jagger or Rod Stewart-like charismatic frontman became one of the world's premier live attractions.

The 1967 'Games For May' concert saw Floyd using the Azimuth Co-ordinator PA system, which enabled them to shift their sound around venues and thereby grant it a new spatial dimension. For audiences still used to bands making do with the crummy PA of the local Odeon or Corn Exchange, it was a revelation.

By the Ummagumma Tour, Floyd were so focused on the optimal performance of their music that they dispensed with support acts because their equipment tended to get in the way of Mason's massive drum kit and Waters' theatrics. On the Atom Heart Mother Tour, it was estimated that the band's perfectionism cost them about £2,000 per performance courtesy of their insistence upon having a choir and brass section to recreate that album's suite faithfully.

## Bigger, Better, Faster, More

With the Dark Side Of The Moon Tour, the band set a new benchmark in lavish spectacle with dry ice, flares, rising platforms, mobile spotlights, strobes and lasers. The story of Pink Floyd live then became an equipment arms race. With each tour there was a new talking point for the fans revolving around the latest outlandish addition to their stagecraft.

The In The Flesh Tour to promote *Animals* saw Floyd commission typically grotesque cartoons from Ralph Steadman shown on a 17-foot tower as well as giant inflatables, including a version of Algie, the plastic pig that had famously become untethered over Battersea Power Station

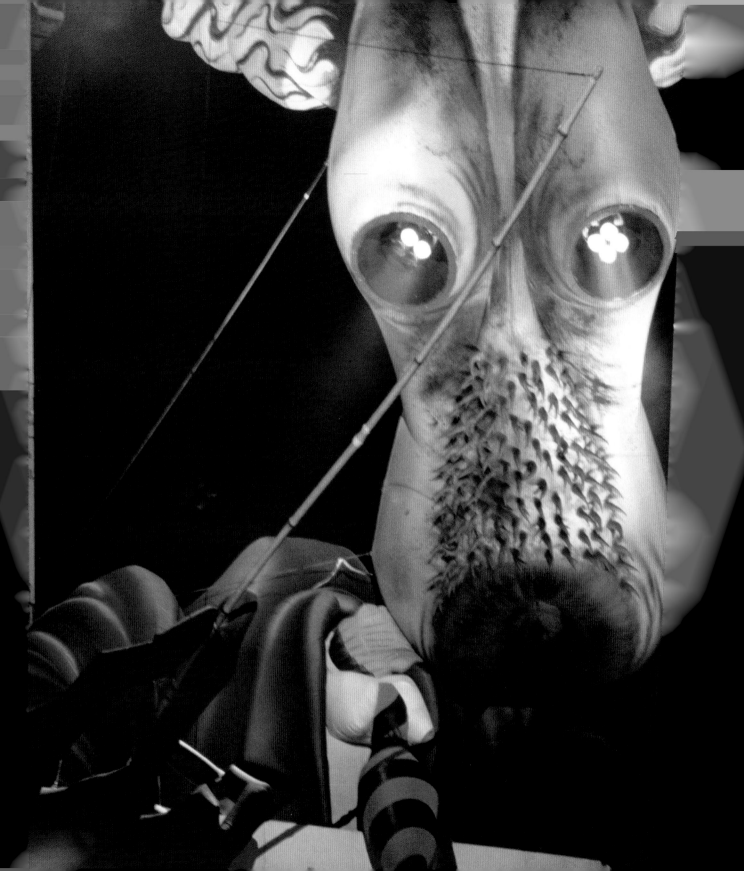

during that album's cover shoot. There were more grotesque cartoons – this time by Gerald Scarfe – and giant inflatables in performances of *The Wall*, but the crowning glory and conceptual masterstroke was that, as Floyd performed that album, a wall would be built in front of them which was then demolished at the end.

## Continuing To Dazzle

Even after the rupture of Floyd, the two separate parties continued to cleave to the stagecraft that had always been important to them when together. Waters' Radio K.A.O.S. Tour enabled audience members to speak to him on the stage from a telephone box. Floyd's A Momentary Lapse Of Reason Tour was also lavish – and featured the *Animals'* flying pig with a pair of testicles as a means to get round the restrictions arising from Waters' legal action. Floyd toured *A Momentary Lapse Of Reason* for three years, making vast profits despite the nervousness of investors over Waters' suit.

While that and The Division Bell Tour may have been viewed as ersatz by Waters fans, the latter at least saw Floyd go out with a bang: the corporate sponsorship enabled three stages, two Boeing 747s, two Skyship 600 airships and a colossal mirror ball, a fitting finale for a group who had always provided a splendid night out.

'OUR ATTITUDE TOWARDS GETTING IT RIGHT WITH THE BEST PA, BEST LIGHTING SYSTEM, HAS RUBBED OFF ON MANY OTHER PEOPLE.'

DAVID GILMOUR

'IN THE
FUTURE,
GROUPS
ARE GOING
TO HAVE
TO OFFER
MORE
THAN A
POP SHOW.'
SYD
BARRETT

'I WAS ALWAYS INTERESTED IN ... HOW TO FILL THE SPACE BETWEEN THE AUDIENCE AND THE IDEA WITH MORE THAN JUST GUITARS AND VOCALS.'

ROGER WATERS

STORMER

# BEYOND FLOYD

'IT'S NOT ANYWHERE IN MY LIST OF THINGS I OUGHT TO THINK ABOUT.'
DAVID GILMOUR ON PINK FLOYD

**T**he Division Bell caused a couple of ripples beyond the unannounced demise of the band. March 1995 saw its sensual track 'Marooned' win a Grammy for the Best Rock Instrumental Performance. Meanwhile, P*U*L*S*E was a double live set from the album's tour that included a complete performance of The Dark Side Of The Moon. Perplexingly, the 22-minute 1994 pre-concert recording 'Soundscape' was only to be found on the album's cassette version. After that, Floyd fans would have to content themselves with archive releases and solo work.

## Floyd From The Vaults

The 1995 EP *London '66-'67* delighted many fans of the Barrett
era by including the full-length version of 'Interstellar Overdrive' that
was excerpted in *Tonite Let's All Make Love In London* plus the
jam 'Nick's Boogie'. The footage of this was released in 2005. *Is
There Anybody Out There? The Wall Live 1980–81* (2000) was
compiled from 16 hours of material recorded at performances at
London's Earl's Court. In 2001 came the double-CD *Echoes: The
Best Of Pink Floyd*. It was the first well-received Floyd compilation.
*A Collection Of Great Dance Songs* (1981), for instance, had
annoyed fans with edits and a re-recorded version of 'Money'
made necessary by the failure to license the original. Of course,
for a band who had mostly disdained singles and some of whose
finest works occupied entire vinyl sides of albums, a best-of set
was almost a contradiction in terms, but this compilation touched
most of the bases by its inclusion of the obvious tracks from the
versions of Floyd led by Barrett, Waters and Gilmour.

Solo releases included Wright's 1996 album *Broken China*,
which movingly dealt with the depression suffered by the
keyboardist's third wife, Mildred. Sinéad O'Connor was guest
vocalist on two of the tracks.

## An Unexpected Memoir

Nick Mason didn't release any solo work. Although he has acted
as producer for plenty of artists, the 1981 LP *Nick Mason's
Fictitious Sports* was not by him at all but really a Carla Bley
album on which he drummed and produced. This and his

# 'PEOPLE KEEP ASKING ME WHEN PINK FLOYD ARE GOING TO MAKE ANOTHER RECORD, BUT I HONESTLY DON'T KNOW.'

RICHARD WRIGHT

almost parodic 'ordinary bloke' persona made it all the more surprising that he should be the Pink Floyd member to publish a memoir of his time in the band. Then again, perhaps it's not so surprising: it's a startling statistic that he is the only band member to have played on their every album. Considering all the unpleasantness that has marked Floyd's career, *Inside Out: A Personal History Of Pink Floyd* (2004) was nothing like as revelatory as it could have been. However, it had plenty of interesting or funny anecdotes and pictures from the drummer's personal archive.

## Two Sorts Of Honour

In November 2003, David Gilmour accepted a CBE from the Queen. The official reason was for services to music but his known generosity probably paid a part: when selling a house for £3.6 million in 2002, he simply passed the money on to housing charity Crisis.

Pink Floyd were inducted into the Rock And Roll Hall Of Fame in January 1996. It was a predictably depressing display from a fragmented, bitter group. Waters didn't bother turning up, while Mason participated in collecting the award but not in the version of 'Wish You Were Here' performed by Gilmour, Wright and the Smashing Pumpkins' Billy Corgan. It hardly augured well for future Floyd activity of any sort.

'PINK FLOYD HAVE BEEN DOING WELL FOR A LONG TIME.'

THE QUEEN WHEN PRESENTING DAVID GILMOUR HIS CBE

# WISH YOU WERE HERE

A fter Pink Floyd fractured in 1968, Syd Barrett would release only two more albums in his lifetime, both of which were disturbing, as not only his songs but also the bewildered way he performed them seemed to trace a disintegrating mind.

## Splendid Isolation

Following *The Madcap Laughs* (1970) and *Barrett* (also 1970), the Crazy Diamond became a recluse, eventually going back to Cambridge where his protective family and vast wealth ensured he could lead a low-profile life, if not recover mental equilibrium.

# WISH YOU WERE HERE

'SYD WAS THE GUIDING LIGHT OF THE EARLY BAND LINE-UP.'
PINK FLOYD STATEMENT ON SYD BARRETT

After Pink Floyd fractured in 1968, Syd Barrett would release only two more albums in his lifetime, both of which were disturbing, as not only his songs but also the bewildered way he performed them seemed to trace a disintegrating mind.

## Splendid Isolation

Following *The Madcap Laughs* (1970) and *Barrett* (also 1970), the Crazy Diamond became a recluse, eventually going back to Cambridge where his protective family and vast wealth ensured he could lead a low-profile life, if not recover mental equilibrium.

However, the ghost of his presence and the debt owed to his original vision runs through the history of Pink Floyd. It was therefore only fitting that Roger Waters said from the stage on 2 July 2005, '…we're doing this for everyone who's not here, but particularly, of course, for Syd.' The occasion was – unbelievably – a performance by a Pink Floyd containing Gilmour, Mason, Waters and Wright.

## Conscience-Led Reunion

For Live 8, his sequel to Live Aid, Bob Geldof decided to try to reunify a splintered heritage rock act like he had with Led Zeppelin and The Who at the original 1985 event. When Gilmour turned Geldof down, it was Waters who persuaded the guitarist it was a good idea. Many people have suspected Waters' socialist values to be spurious, the over-compensation of a deeply flawed human being. However, his social conscience is probably the only thing that could have persuaded him to reunite with his ex-colleagues.

Consequently, 205,000 people in a darkened Hyde Park and a global television audience of millions saw Floyd – all now grey, Gilmour bald – perform powerful versions of 'Breathe', 'Money', 'Wish You Were Here' and 'Comfortably Numb'. That Waters looked ecstatic and humble was consistent with the general opinion that he had become a much more easy-going fellow.

## Sweet But Final

There was to be, though, no long-term reunion. Waters would only speak of doing it as a one-off for another special occasion. Gilmour wouldn't speak of it at all, stating that the experience had been 'like sleeping with your ex-wife'.

In any case, it all became academic on 15 September 2008 when Richard Wright passed away after a short battle with cancer. Pink Floyd had already lost family on 7 July 2006 when Syd Barrett died, pancreatic cancer the cause.

This all made the group's fans even more grateful for the Live 8 appearance. With Pink Floyd definitively passing into history, they could treasure both Waters' tribute to Barrett and the group hug that had climaxed their performance.

It was a pleasing endnote for a musical legend.

*'It was an extraordinarily moving experience for me and if that's the way we draw a line under Pink Floyd, so be it.'*

*Roger Waters on Live 8*

*'Any squabbles Roger and the band have had in the past are so petty in this context.'*

*David Gilmour on Live 8*

# FURTHER INFORMATION

## PINK FLOYD VITAL INFO

### Syd Barrett

**Name:** Roger Keith 'Syd' Barrett
**Born:** 6 January 1946; **Died:** 7 July 2006
**Birth Place:** Cambridge, England
**Role:** Lead vocalist and guitarist

### Nick Mason

**Name:** Nicholas Berkeley 'Nick' Mason
**Birth Date:** 27 January 1944
**Birth Place:** Edgbaston, Birmingham, England
**Role:** Drummer

### Roger Waters

**Name:** George Roger Waters
**Birth Date:** 6 September 1943
**Birth Place:** Great Bookham, Surrey, England
**Role:** Vocalist and bassist

### Richard Wright

**Name:** Richard William 'Rick' Wright
**Born:** 28 July 1943; **Died:** 15 September 2008
**Birth Place:** Hatch End, Middlesex, England
**Role:** Keyboardist

### David Gilmour

**Name:** David Jon Gilmour
**Birth Date:** 6 March 1946
**Birth Place:** Cambridge, England
**Role:** Vocalist and guitarist

# DISCOGRAPHY

## Selected Albums

*The Piper at the Gates of Dawn* (1967)

*A Saucerful Of Secrets* (1968)

*Soundtrack from the Film More* (1969)

*Ummagumma* (1969)

*Atom Heart Mother* (1970)

*Meddle* (1971)

*Relics* (1971)

*Obscured by Clouds* (1972)

*The Dark Side of the Moon* (1973)

*A Nice Pair* (1974)

*Wish You Were Here* (1975)

*Animals* (1977)

*The Wall* (1979)

*The Final Cut* (1983)

*A Momentary Lapse of Reason* (1987)

*Delicate Sound of Thunder* (1988)

*The Division Bell* (1994)

*Pulse* (1995)

*Is There Anybody Out There* (2000)

*Echoes: The Best of Pink Floyd* (2001)

*A Foot in the Door-The Best of Pink Floyd* (2011)

## Selected Singles

**1967:** 'See Emily Play' (UK No. 6)
**1979:** 'Another Brick in the Wall (Part II)' (UK No. 2)

# AWARDS

## Grammy Awards

**1995:**    Best Rock Instrumental Performance 'Marooned'

**1999:**    Hall of Fame *The Dark Side of the Moon*

## Ivor Novello Awards

**1992:**    Outstanding Contribution to British Music

## Juno Awards

**1981:**    International Single of the Year 'Another Brick in the Wall'

            International Album of the Year *The Wall*

## MTV Video Music Awards

**1988:**    Best Concept Video 'Learning To Fly'

## Polar Music Prize

**2008**:    Contribution to Modern Music

## *Q* Music Awards

**1994:**    Best Live Act

# SELECTED TOURS

**Pink Floyd World Tour:** February–December 1968; Europe and North America

**The Man and The Journey Tour:** April–September 1969; England and The Netherlands

**Atom Heart Mother World Tour:** September 1970–October 1971; Worldwide

**Meddle Tour:** October–November 1971; North America

**Dark Side Of The Moon Tour:** January 1972–November 1973; Worldwide

**French Summer Tour:** June–December 1974; France

**British Winter Tour:** November–December 1974; UK

**Wish You Were Here Tour:** April–July 1975; North America

**In the Flesh Tour:** January–July 1977; Europe and North America

**The Wall Tour:** February 1980–June 1981; LA, New York, Dortmund and London

**A Momentary Lapse of Reason Tour:** September 1987–July 1989; June 1990; Worldwide

**The Division Bell Tour:** March-October 1994; North America and Europe

**The Wall Live (Concert Tour):** September 2010–September 2013; Worldwide (Roger Waters only)

# ONLINE

**www.pinkfloyd.com:** The Floyd's official site.

**@PinkFloydOnline:** Follow Twitter updates from Pink Floyd.

**www.facebook.com/pinkfloyd:** Fan site is run by EMI. Over 23 million likes.

# BIOGRAPHIES

## Sean Egan

Londoner Sean Egan has contributed to, among others, *Billboard*, *Book Collector*, *Classic Rock*, *Record Collector*, *Tennis World*, *Total Film*, *Uncut* and RollingStone.com. He has written or edited nineteen books, including works on The Beatles, Jimi Hendrix, The Rolling Stones, *Coronation Street*, Manchester United and Tarzan. His critically acclaimed novel *Sick of Being Me* was published in 2003, while *Don't Mess with the Best*, his 2008 collection of short stories, carried cover endorsements from Booker Prize winners Stanley Middleton and David Storey.

## Jerry Ewing

Jerry Ewing (Foreword) is the editor of *Classic Rock Presents Prog*. He set up *Classic Rock* for Dennis Publishing in 1998 and prior to that was deputy editor of *Metal Hammer*. He still writes for both *Classic Rock* and *Metal Hammer*, as well as *Maxim*, *Bizarre* and *Rocks* magazine in Germany. He has several books to his name on the likes of AC/DC, Led Zeppelin and Metallica and has made a raft of appearances on TV and DVD, as well as doing voice-over work. He has also presented radio shows on Total Rock for 10 years.

# PICTURE CREDITS